"This book is short but filled with wis[dom?]... come from someone who has personally traveled this road... filled with God's Word and the heart and tone of a skilled caregiver who gently unpacks the confusion, guilt, shame, fear, and grief that so often accompany the pain of abortion. Additionally, it's filled with the grace, truth, and transparency needed to walk others out of the dark and into the light of God's forgiveness and freedom."

> **Brad Bigney,** Lead Pastor, Grace Fellowship Church, Florence, KY; ACBC certified counselor; author of *Gospel Treason*

"In *Moving Forward after Abortion*, Camille comes alongside readers as a wise Christian sister—one who knows what it's like to wade through the tumultuous wake of grief and trauma. As she humbly recounts her own post-abortion journey, readers are graciously invited to embrace the same gospel-centered comfort that brought her aching heart healing and hope."

> **Christine Chappell,** Author of *Midnight*; host, *Hope + Help Podcast*, Institute for Biblical Counseling & Discipleship; certified biblical counselor

"Saturated in Scripture, Camille's book offers real biblical solutions for dealing with pain, depression, anxiety, anger, guilt, and grief that accompany abortion. She encourages readers to get to the root of their sin and enjoy the forgiveness and restoration found only in the gospel of Jesus Christ. God's grace, mercy, and compassion alone offer true healing and hope!"

> **Georgia Purdom,** Vice President of Educational Content and Director of *Answers for Women* Conferences, Answers in Genesis

"*Moving Forward after Abortion* is life-giving water for your parched soul. Camille helps uncover the lies post-abortive women and men believe and then replaces those lies with the truth. Take this little book and let it lead you to the One who is Living Water."

> **Kathleen Shanks,** Executive Director, New Path Pregnancy Resource Centers

"Camille has powerfully provided a gospel-saturated, healing resource for anyone carrying the pain of abortion. Her vulnerable story of trauma and choices, combined with a message of compassionate help and scriptural hope, will help readers exchange pain for God's redemptive love to find freedom and restoration."

Lisa Appelo, Author of *Life Can Be Good Again*

"*Moving Forward after Abortion* is a window into how the Lord forgives, heals, and restores a woman after an abortion. Camille's writing is clear and raw, and her transparency often led me to tears. This book spills over with Scripture, biblical wisdom, book recommendations, and hope. I have never read a book like this and cannot recommend it highly enough."

Rosaria Butterfield, Former tenured professor of English and Women's Studies, Syracuse University; author of *The Gospel Comes with a House Key* and *Five Lies of our Anti-Christian Age*

"I broke down crying multiple times as I read this book. It is moving, biblical, informative, tender, kind, and hope-filled. *Moving Forward after Abortion* is a balm to the broken soul and points us to the powerful grace of God in Christ Jesus. God does not want anyone living in the shackles of sin and shame. My heart is bursting with joy and my eyes are filled with tears as I reflect upon the stories and truth that Camille shares. I cannot recommend this book enough. I want everyone to read it."

Sean Perron, Associate Pastor, First Baptist Jacksonville; ACBC certified counselor; author

"This book is a great resource for counselors, churches, and pregnancy centers for women and men needing hope and healing after abortion. The author shares her own journey of how she found true healing in Jesus and the Word of God. The reflective questions at the end of each chapter are great. I wholeheartedly recommend this book!"

MaryAnn Ambroselli, Former Executive Director and current board of directors chairperson, Ventura County Pregnancy Center; certified biblical counselor, Healing Hearts Ministries International

MOVING FORWARD AFTER ABORTION

MOVING FORWARD AFTER ABORTION

FINDING COMFORT IN GOD

Camille Cates

New
Growth
Press

newgrowthpress.com

New Growth Press, Greensboro, NC 27401
newgrowthpress.com
Copyright © 2023 by Camille Cates

Cover Design: Studio Gearbox, studiogearbox.com
Interior Typesetting and eBook: Lisa Parnell, lparnellbookservices.com

ISBN: 978-1-64507-312-3 (Print)
ISBN: 978-1-64507-313-0 (eBook)

Library of Congress Cataloging-in-Publication Data on file

Printed in the United States of America

30 29 28 27 26 25 24 23   1 2 3 4 5

Dedication

*This book is dedicated to Teresa Rinker,
who shared her own abortion story with me and showed
me through God's Word that Jesus gives us "beauty for
ashes, a joyous blessing instead of mourning, and festive
praise instead of despair" (Isaiah 61:3).*

CONTENTS

START MOVING FORWARD
(READ THIS FIRST)

What does someone who has had an abortion look like? She looks like a middle-aged mom shopping in the grocery store, a college professor teaching a class on ethics, a young woman taking your order in the drive-through, a pastor's wife, or a woman leading your Bible study. She looks like you and she looks like me. And along with every woman who has had an abortion, there is a man who was the father of her baby. It's important to acknowledge that abortion impacts men too, even if that impact manifests differently.

For the purpose of this book, we will focus on women, but men may also find help from the biblical truths presented. If your husband is the father of your aborted baby, or the father of an aborted baby from another relationship, you may want to read this book at the same time and talk about what you are learning. Many couples have found comfort and healing from God as they revisit an abortion experience together. If you find yourselves stuck or in a conflict that you cannot resolve on your own, see your pastor or a biblical counselor for help.

Since 1999, I have been working with women who have been left with hurt, confusion, and unanswered questions after an abortion. Each of their stories is different, and the problems they have faced afterward vary. Yet the solution for those problems can be found in the same source, the Bible. When I needed healing after my own abortion, what helped me immensely was immersing myself in God's Word. It had a profound impact on me and was truly life-changing. Before studying God's Word, I didn't realize all the areas of my life that had been impacted by my abortion, and I hadn't processed the circumstances leading up to it.

I ended up going through a wonderful Bible study titled *Binding Up the Brokenhearted*, written by Sue Liljenberg. As I did the study, I was paired up with a mature Christian mentor who had also had an abortion and experienced God's healing work in her life afterward. When you finish reading this book, I recommend going through the same Bible study.[1]

I found it incredibly comforting to walk alongside another woman who had been in my shoes. It also helped me to go through a Bible study written by a woman who was well-acquainted with the many emotions that come after an abortion. I hope and pray that you feel comforted as you read this book, not only by my words as a woman who has had an abortion, but by God's Word. The Bible truly has answers for aching hearts and mixed-up minds. When you look to God's inerrant, authoritative, and sufficient Word, you will discover astonishing displays of his grace, mercy, love, and forgiveness and encounter the power to restore that which sin has broken.

Before we explore some common questions people have after an abortion, I want to recognize that readers of this book are in different places spiritually. Some have already turned to Jesus to save them from their sins. Some have not yet turned to him for salvation. Wherever you are, spiritually speaking, I urge you to use this time to search out the God of the Bible. Do you know him as your loving Creator and Heavenly Father? Or does he seem distant and impersonal to you? Consider Psalm 145:18, which says, "The LORD is near to all who call on him, to all who call on him in truth."

If you know that you are not yet a Christian, you can simply pray, asking God to reveal himself to you through his Word. Tell him, "Lord, I am calling on you in truth right now. I need to know you and to know that you are near." If you feel like something in your life is keeping you from God, reflect on Isaiah 59:1, which says, "Behold, the LORD's hand is not shortened, that it cannot save, or his ear dull, that it cannot hear." God's ears and arms are open. His hand is powerful to save. He will hear you when you call. Indeed, God's nature is to listen and to save when we call on him (Psalm 50:15, Lamentations 3:55–57). Will you open your heart to him as you read this book?

Perhaps you are a Christian. Christians will also have varying experiences regarding their abortions. Some had an abortion before coming to know Christ. And others, like me, had an abortion as a Christian. After my abortion, one of the biggest questions I had was "How could I be a Christian and choose to have an abortion?" If you too were a Christian at the time of your abortion, it's important to understand that Christians are still tempted to sin and give into sin, including some of the most grievous of sins (Romans 7:21–25). But if you have turned to Jesus Christ for salvation, God is faithful to forgive your sins—all of them. He further promises his followers that in heaven, "we shall be like him, because we shall see him as he is" (1 John 3:2).

A FEW WORDS ABOUT HOW TO APPROACH THIS BOOK

First, in the past, you may have had Bible verses thrown at you in unhelpful or even painful ways. Sometimes, well-meaning pastors or Christian counselors can dole out a few verses like a doctor prescribing medicine: "Take two verses and call me in the morning." As you read this book, you will see that I frequently cite Scripture. My desire is that the profound insights and deep truths of God's Word will encourage you and strengthen your faith. I have also included real-life stories and practical examples so you can see how the Bible applies to your life.

Second, no single book can address every experience of every woman who has ever had an abortion. So, throughout this book, I'm recommending further readings for those who feel the need for more in-depth help on a particular subject. Most of the recommendations are short, easy reads, but are tremendously helpful and provide much personal application.

Third, reflecting on your own abortion story will not be easy. But it is important if you want to move forward after your abortion and find comfort in God. I invite you to go at your own pace. Take breaks when you feel overwhelmed. You may want to talk to a pastor, trusted friend, or counselor about what you're reading.

Finally, let me offer you some encouragement. God has led you to pick up this book at just the right time because he wants you to know that he is near (Psalm 119:151). Also, in chapter 1, I have shared my abortion story with you. I hope and pray that it gives you hope as you learn about our loving and merciful Savior, Jesus. If your abortion has weighed you down or left you questioning God's perfect love for you, consider this precious promise in Matthew 11:28–29: "Come to me, all of you who are weary and carry heavy burdens, and I will give you rest. Take my yoke upon you. Let me teach you, because I am humble and gentle at heart, and you will find rest for your souls" (NLT). I found rest in Jesus after my abortion experience. You can too.

Chapter 1

WHO CAN I TURN TO AFTER MY ABORTION?

A month shy of turning seventeen, I missed my period for the first time. Terrified to tell my parents, I turned to my best friend who went with me to a local women's clinic for a pregnancy test. Anxiously awaiting the results, I couldn't think about anything else. Minutes seemed like hours.

It's interesting how those same two little lines that appear on a positive pregnancy test are viewed very differently depending on a person's desires. For the woman who is eagerly trying to start a family, those two lines bring sheer joy. But that same positive test result provokes panic in a woman who wasn't expecting to become pregnant.

When the woman at the clinic stepped into the room and told me, "It's positive," my heart dropped into my stomach. Suddenly, my mind went racing, wondering how my parents would react. Eventually, I had to confess to them that I was pregnant. My mother's immediate response was to ask me if I wanted to have an abortion. I was shocked. Both of my parents professed to be Christians. I too professed faith in Christ, even though I was sexually promiscuous. I told my mom, "No. I want to keep my baby." Thankfully, my parents supported my decision.

Six months later, I graduated from high school, and three months after that I gave birth to a beautiful baby girl and named her Lauren. After she was born, I tried getting my life together. I started college, worked a couple of part-time jobs, began attending church regularly, and took care of Lauren the best I could. But I was still looking for a romantic relationship.

HERE WE GO AGAIN

Eventually, I became involved in a relationship with another man. He seemed like a nice guy from a decent family with similar values to mine. We became sexually active, and I became pregnant again. Lauren wasn't even a year old yet. My mom and dad soon found out. This time, they really put pressure on us to have an abortion. They slammed me with questions, "How are you going to take care of two babies? You are working two jobs while going to school. Does he even have a job? How are you going to make this work? It's not fair to Lauren."

My parents' skepticism created doubt in my mind. I started contemplating what the future might look like if we kept the baby. Feeling unsettled, my boyfriend and I began tossing around the idea of an abortion. However, we never had the chance to make that decision together. He did something that turned my world upside down and altered the course of our lives.

One evening, I left Lauren in his care while I went to work. During my shift, my mom came into my workplace and told me, "We have to go to the hospital. Something has happened to Lauren." When I arrived at the hospital, the staff wouldn't let me back to see Lauren. As I sat in the waiting room of the ER, I listened to the details of my boyfriend's account of what happened. Later on, he and I were both interviewed by Child Protective Services. Something wasn't adding up. But I couldn't figure out what was going on. I spent the night laying on the waiting room floor, floating in and out of sleep, exhausted from worry, yet eagerly anticipating news about Lauren's condition. I was hopeful that the hospital staff would come out any moment and let me go back to her room to see her.

The next morning, Lauren's pediatrician arrived at the hospital to examine her. She brought me into Lauren's hospital room for a consultation. I saw Lauren lying there unconscious in the hospital bed, her little body and head showed signs of bruising. It was then that her doctor informed me that Lauren had been sexually assaulted and shaken to death. My little girl was gone. Eventually, my boyfriend turned himself in to the police. I had to face the fact that I was still pregnant with his baby, and now I was alone.

I found myself wondering how I could possibly carry the baby of the man who had killed my child. Many women who have been raped ask themselves a similar question: "How can I carry the baby of the man who assaulted me?" In that moment, my greatest fear was having to someday tell this child what his father had done and why he was no longer in our lives.

Trying to justify having an abortion, I began questioning God, then pleading with him, and ultimately bargaining with him. I prayed, "God, I know abortion is wrong, but you know how hard all of this is for me. I can't go through with this pregnancy. My situation is unique. God, this one time, having an abortion has to be okay with you."

Only four days after burying Lauren, I had the abortion. In the days that followed, darkness overtook me. I felt so lost and alone. Every night I went to bed begging God not to let me wake up. Then, the next day would dawn.

IN NEED OF MY SAVIOR

For the following two years, I ambled along, barely functioning. I lived for partying with my friends—sleeping all day and staying up all night—drinking, doing drugs, and having sex with anyone who was willing. The daytime repulsed me, leaving me no place to hide and no way to cover up what I was going through. Completely shattered, I turned to anything and anyone to numb my pain.

Until God brought me to the end of myself.

One night, I went out with a guy I had dated back in high school. He wanted to have sex. But something in my heart simply snapped. I was done with that lifestyle. I realized that if I kept making the same wrong choices, I was going to get the same miserable results. So, I told him no and goodbye, and I left.

When I got home, I hurried inside to my bedroom and flung myself on the bed. I cried out, "God, I am finished! All this time, I have been chasing after every single relationship but the one I have with you. I want you and you alone."

The next day, I began living differently, seeking after the Lord, and longing to be close to him every moment. Eventually, God brought a young man into my life who had just graduated from seminary and was headed into youth ministry. He knew about my past and didn't care. This man genuinely loved me, even after finding out about my abortion. I married him and began serving alongside him in ministry.

But my past abortion haunted me. Ultimately, God led me to find biblical healing and renewal through the Scriptures. One summer, about three years into our marriage, I attended a women's conference with several ladies from my church. It was at that event that I came across a ministry specifically focused on helping women struggling with post-abortion trauma. I went through an in-depth Bible study and God used it to powerfully transform my life! Dealing with the events leading up to my abortion, processing the abortion itself, and working through the many thoughts and emotions that came afterward allowed me to apply God's truth to my heart. This brought me tremendous healing. When I had finished the study, my husband even told me, "You are a completely different woman."

Yet something was holding me back from living in total freedom. While I had come to believe that Jesus had forgiven all my sins—including my abortion—I was concerned about what other people would think about me if they knew. Still, the love of Christ compelled me, and I could no longer stay silent about what he had done for me. I recognized that other women were hurting and brokenhearted over their abortions. They too needed healing as I once did. I was excited about being able to freely share this good news with them.

My husband and I prayed about sharing my story with our pastor and his wife first—even though we feared that it could cost my husband his job. I was anxious about what our pastor, his wife, and others at church would think. Perhaps you can relate. Have you gone to a pastor or counselor to talk? Or have you been trying to work up the nerve to speak to someone (anyone) about your abortion? Maybe those you trusted with your secret didn't know how to truly help, and you've been left with even more hurt and confusion.

Thankfully, my pastor, his wife, and our church lovingly embraced me and encouraged me to share my testimony with other people who were hurting after abortion. But you may be in a place where you are not sure you can ever tell anyone about what happened. Simply having this book in your possession might induce a little panic. Have you hidden it under the bed or in the back of a drawer, or placed it under lock and key so that no one will find it? Do you feel nauseous at the thought of even saying the word *abortion*? I get it. I was once terribly afraid of what others would think if they knew that I had an abortion.

FOLLOW IN HER FOOTSTEPS

Your secrecy about your abortion is understandable. Our culture constantly fights over the issue. Women and men who have been involved in an abortion can feel caught in the fray as social media bullets fly and news brief bombs explode between the political left and right. Jesus wants you to know that you can find refuge and safety from the culture war by coming to him (Psalm 46:1–3).

One particular woman in Scripture boldly believed she could find healing in Jesus—a healing she so desperately needed. If she could just get through the crowd unnoticed and touch the hem of his garment, she knew she could be healed. So, she snuck up on the Savior in the middle of a pressing crowd and reached out her hand.

We learn more of the story in Mark 5. It says, "And there was a woman who had had a discharge of blood for twelve years, and who had suffered much under many physicians, and had spent all that she had, and was no better but rather grew worse. She had heard the reports about Jesus and came up behind him in the crowd and touched his garment. For she said, 'If I touch even his garments, I will be made well'" (Mark 5:25–28).

This woman had suffered for more than a decade, buried under a heap of societal shame and isolated from others because of the law regarding her bloody discharge. For all that she had tried to do to alleviate her ailments—physical, emotional, and perhaps, even spiritual—she had grown worse, not better. Her condition—which violated the hygienic practices under the Jewish law—had made her "unclean" to everyone around her (Leviticus 15:25–30). That is, everyone but Jesus.

She needed a Savior, so she dared to come to Jesus and reach out to him. This time, her efforts to seek help bore fruit. She pressed in close to Jesus, and his power went out. She was finally healed.

The Scriptures tell us, "And immediately the flow of blood dried up, and she felt in her body that she was healed of her disease. And Jesus, perceiving in himself that power had gone out from him, immediately turned about in the crowd and said, 'Who touched my garments?'" (Mark 5:29–30).

The woman probably thought Jesus was summoning her to condemn her for touching him, not to comfort her and give her peace. We read, "But the woman, knowing what had happened to her, came in fear and trembling and fell down before him and told him the whole truth. And he said to her, 'Daughter, your faith has made you well; go in peace, and be healed of your disease'" (Mark 5:33–34).

After she had been healed, Jesus called her out in the middle of a huge crowd. Consider for a moment that he is all-knowing. Christ wasn't clueless about who had touched him. He was drawing her out, not to shame her, but to bring her closer, acknowledge her pain and suffering, and provide her with peace.

Right now, you may feel like this woman did initially. Take some time to think about her story. Then, think about your own. How long have you been suffering from shame, isolation, or other emotional torments from your abortion? What lengths have you taken to be rid of the pain and guilt of your past? Are you afraid of what others in the church will think about you? Are you fearful that God has already condemned you, or is somehow punishing you for your abortion?

Be encouraged that the only one in the crowd of people who had the right to condemn her didn't. Jesus didn't call her forward to shame her, but to change her.

She recognized him as her only hope for healing, and she risked everything to receive it. What about you? Are you willing to boldly approach God for the healing you need? Will you come to him?

FOR REFLECTION

1. How long have you been suffering from shame, isolation, or other mental and emotional torments from your abortion?

2. What lengths have you taken to be rid of the pain and guilt of your past?

Read through these passages and reflect on the benefits of seeking God in vulnerability and humility. Write out one or two truths and how you will apply them to your life.

- John 3:16–18
- Romans 8:1–6

FURTHER READING

- Edward T. Welch, *Shame Interrupted: How God Lifts the Pain of Worthlessness and Rejection* (Greensboro, NC: New Growth Press, 2012).
- Edward T. Welch, *A Small Book about Why We Hide: How Jesus Rescues Us from Insecurity, Regret, Failure, and Shame* (Greensboro, NC: New Growth Press, 2021).

Chapter 2

IS GOD GOING TO PUNISH ME FOR MY ABORTION?

Originally, God made a world that was free from pain, suffering, and punishment—a pristine paradise. In the first book of the Bible, Genesis, it says, "And God saw everything that he had made, and behold, it was very good" (Genesis 1:31a). While God created a perfect world, that perfection was short-lived when the first man and woman—Adam and Eve—decided to rebel against God's good plan for them (Genesis 3:1–19). Because God is holy, righteous, and just, he had to address their rebellion.

God hates sin not only because it is offensive to his holiness, but because it is destructive to humankind (Romans 5:12). Sin ruins people's lives, both on an individual level and a societal level. Therefore, sin must be addressed.

THE GREAT EXCHANGE

Ever since Adam and Eve rejected God's sovereign rule in favor of self-rule, their offspring have done the same, with disastrous results (Romans 1:18–32). Scripture says, "For although they knew God, they did not honor him as God or give thanks to him, but they became futile in their thinking and their foolish hearts were darkened. Claiming to be wise, they became fools, and exchanged the glory of the immortal God for images resembling mortal man and birds and animals and creeping things" (Romans 1:21–23). The passage goes on to state, "they exchanged the truth about God for a lie and worshiped and served the creature rather than the Creator" (Romans 1:25).

That unwise exchange needed a reversal so that sinners could be made right with God and live in open fellowship with their Creator. But the only one who could undo it had to be both human and sinless (Hebrews 2:14–18). Because Jesus came to earth as a human being who was tempted by sin but never gave into it, he was the perfect, unblemished sacrifice for sinners (Hebrews 9:13–14). Jesus was able to make the great exchange necessary to save people from sin and death.

God knew that you could never pay the penalty for your sin. So, in his mercy and kindness, God the Father sent his Son, Jesus, to redeem his people from the curse of the law by becoming a curse for us in his death on the cross (Galatians 3:13). Isaiah 53:5 describes what Jesus went through as he was crucified, "But he was pierced for our transgressions; he was crushed for our iniquities; upon him was the chastisement that brought us peace, and with his wounds we are healed."

Go back to Isaiah 53:5 and underline the phrases "pierced for our transgressions" and "crushed for our iniquities." Next, draw a square around "upon him was the chastisement" and "with his wounds." Then, circle the phrases "brought us peace" and "we are healed."

Why would Jesus take on our sin as if it were his? Why would he be willing to be condemned, then suffer and die in our place? It was so you and I could have peace, healing, and most importantly, eternal life in and through him (Isaiah 53:4–12; John 6:40). Though God despises sin, he also loves his creation (John 3:16).

Out of love, Jesus was willing to fully absorb God's wrath for your sin—your annoyance with a particular family member, your bad attitude at work, your unkindness toward your neighbor, and yes, even your abortion—bearing it upon the cross (Romans 5:8–9). In doing so, Jesus made a wise and good exchange on behalf of repentant sinners.

The Bible tells us, "For God made Christ, who never sinned, to be the offering for our sin, so that we could be made right with God through Christ" (2 Corinthians 5:21 NLT). In exchange for your sin (including the sin of abortion), Jesus offers his perfect righteousness to you. As a result, if you accept this exchange, your sin is gone, and you stand righteous before God. That is the gospel—the good news—of Jesus!

It is common for a woman who has had an abortion to question whether or not God will punish her for it. Oftentimes, she wonders if he will prevent her from becoming pregnant again. Or, if there has been a pregnancy loss since the abortion, she looks back at that loss and believes God was dishing out his divine wrath toward her. But this is not the heart of our gracious and merciful God.

Regarding any punishment from God after an abortion, those who are in Christ no longer need to fear. It's important to understand that God doesn't punish us as our sins deserve because judgment fell on Jesus on the cross. Psalm 103:10 says, "He does not punish us for all our sins; he does not deal harshly with us, as we deserve" (NLT). If you have put your faith in Christ, you can let go of this fear of punishment because Jesus took the Father's wrath upon himself and bore the punishment for your abortion on your behalf. There is no longer any reason for him to condemn and punish you. According to Romans 8:1–2, God promises, "There is therefore now no condemnation for those who are in Christ Jesus. For the law of the Spirit of life has set you free in Christ Jesus from the law of sin and death." That is good news!

GOD DOESN'T PUNISH HIS CHILDREN, HE DISCIPLINES THEM

When you place your faith in Jesus, God the Father adopts you as his child (Ephesians 1:5). As his child, there is no longer a reason to fear his punishment. For God is not punitive toward his children. Rather, God the Father lovingly disciplines his children.

Proverbs 3:11–12 tells us, "My child, don't reject the LORD's discipline, and don't be upset when he corrects you. For the LORD corrects those he loves, just as a father corrects a child in whom he delights" (NLT). The Bible exhorts us not to despise God's discipline or become weary. Why? Because he takes delight in teaching his children, wanting his best for us. God disciplines us to teach us to be more like him. Consider Hebrews

12:11, which says, "For the moment all discipline seems painful rather than pleasant, but later it yields the peaceful fruit of righteousness to those who have been trained by it."

Think about it this way: have you ever said something in anger in the heat of an argument that you regretted? Perhaps it hurt your friend or loved one badly. Hopefully, the fracture in the relationship caused you to go to the person you sinned against to seek forgiveness and reconciliation. If God uses your sin to convict you and to teach you to be more cautious and gentle with your words, then he has disciplined (or taught) you to be more like Jesus. So, every time you experience God's discipline regarding your sin, it is meant to teach you to become more like Jesus in your thoughts, desires, and actions.

NOW IS THE TIME TO DRAW NEAR TO GOD

Looking back, the pain of losing my daughter Lauren and the conviction I felt after my abortion caused me to turn back to God. He used the painful loss and devastation from my own sin to call me back to him. I drew near to God, he drew near to me, and I learned more about him in the process (James 4:8). God began to teach me more about himself through his Word, how to better deal with the temptation to sin, how to build biblical and healthy relationships, and so much more!

God wants you to draw near to him for healing after your abortion. Psalm 34:18 nudges our hurting hearts to lean into Jesus: "The LORD is near to the brokenhearted and saves the crushed in spirit." Yet you may be protesting, pushing away from God's presence, perplexed that he would allow you to experience suffering at all. Perhaps you struggle with the thought that he could have prevented the circumstances that led up to your abortion—or prevented you from becoming pregnant to begin with. I have to be fair and say, yes, he could have kept you from it all. He could have prevented my suffering, too. But He didn't.

If you are tempted to be embittered toward God, be assured that God is not a sadist who loves to inflict pain upon humanity. He doesn't take pleasure in our suffering, for that would be cruel. And God is not unjust, unfair, or unkind.

Pause and consider God's compassionate nature. Listen to what these verses tell us about God's heart for his people: "Though he brings grief, he also shows compassion because of the greatness of his unfailing love. For he does not enjoy hurting people or causing them sorrow" (Lamentations 3:32–33 NLT; cf. Ezekiel 33:10–11).

Even more, God, through Jesus Christ, entered into our human suffering. Jesus was "a man of sorrows and acquainted with grief" (Isaiah 53:3), so he understands what it is to mourn, to be betrayed, to feel physical pain. And even now he is with you in your suffering to bring you healing and transformation (Psalm 147:3).

Jesus came near to us to comfort us in our brokenness so that we can share the comfort we have received from him with others who are hurting. Scripture says, "Blessed be the God and Father of our Lord Jesus Christ, the Father of mercies and God of all comfort, who comforts us in all our affliction [suffering], so that we may be able to comfort those who are in any affliction, with the comfort with which we ourselves are comforted by God" (2 Corinthians 1:3–4).

God, in his mercy and kindness, doesn't waste the pain and suffering that his children endure. It's not all for naught. He uses both our sin and suffering to reveal more of himself to us. When you realize that God lovingly disciplines his children, it should bring you a sense of peace. No longer should you believe the lie that God is punishing you for your abortion. Instead, you experience freedom as you acknowledge your sins before the Lord and turn to him to grow and change to be more like Christ. And, when God's children reflect his love, peace, kindness, goodness, etc., to the world, he is glorified (John 15:8).

FOR REFLECTION

1. Are you still fearing God's punishment for your abortion? If so, why?

2. How do you see God's loving discipline in your life since your abortion?

Read through these passages and reflect on how you no longer have to fear God's punishment, but can rest in his love, including his loving discipline. Write out one or two truths and how you will apply them to your life.

- 1 John 4:18–19
- Hebrews 12:11

FURTHER READING

- David Powlison, *God's Grace in Your Suffering* (Wheaton, IL: Crossway, 2018).
- William P. Smith, *When Bad Things Happen: Thoughtful Answers to Hard Question* (Greensboro, NC: New Growth Press, 2008).
- Mark Vroegop, *Dark Clouds, Deep Mercy: Discovering God's Grace in Your Lament* (Wheaton, IL: Crossway, 2019).

Chapter 3

WHY CAN'T I
JUST MOVE ON?

Before you get too far into this book, I want to encourage you that this book was written to provide you with a safe place to work through everything surrounding your previous abortion. Just as my story was filled with complexities and trauma, yours may be full of one heartbreaking sorrow after another.

One woman I talked with had been regularly beaten by her ex-boyfriend. Describing the ongoing trauma to me, she recounted one night that he had beaten her to the ground and then started kicking her in the stomach. She was pregnant at the time, and he wasn't happy about it. She decided to have an abortion thinking, *It's better for me to have an abortion than for him to end up killing me in the process of trying to kill the baby*. After she had the abortion, she thought the abuse would stop. It continued.

Another woman I know was happily married and expecting. She discovered her husband was having an affair. He said he wanted to leave her for the other woman. So, she agreed to have an abortion. Not long after, the affair he was having dissolved and the couple stayed married. She lived day after day in her marriage with regret over her abortion and filled with bitterness toward her husband. The abortion, on top of the adultery, took its toll on their marriage.

Yet another woman, visibly shaking as I met with her, conveyed how her obstetrician had told her and her husband the baby she was pregnant with had a severe abnormality. The couple had three other children. Though they knew abortion was wrong, they were scared to face the possibility of parenting a disabled child for the rest of their lives. The trauma of the poor prognosis for their baby had pushed the couple to the edge. She began having panic attacks and nightmares. Her husband was bewildered as to how to help her. They ended up having an abortion. Her panic attacks and nightmares continued long after the abortion, and so did her husband's confusion about how to care for his wife's mental, emotional, and spiritual needs.

Additional trauma, dire situations, or unexpected complications you may have had surrounding your previous pregnancy can make it difficult to move past your abortion. Sorting through all of the tangled thoughts and emotions is overwhelming and exhausting. Where do you even begin? It can be tempting to just keep distancing yourself from it all instead of taking your hurting and confused heart to Jesus and letting him heal your deepest wounds so that you can move forward.

Whether you are living with the trauma of your abortion or other life events that were traumatic, Jesus wants you to find hope and help in him. Though we don't have the time to work through every traumatic event you have experienced, I would encourage you to seek additional help after you finish this book.

ACKNOWLEDGING YOUR ABORTION AS SIN IS HEALING

Whether or not you had other trauma or complexities surrounding your abortion, it can be tempting to try to justify your abortion or shift the blame to someone else. For me, though I had been traumatized by the sexual assault and murder of my daughter, for many years I only focused on that trauma instead of also taking responsibility for my choice. Of course, I absolutely needed to heal from all the wrong that was done to me and my daughter, but I also tried to shift the blame for my abortion solely on my ex-boyfriend for his actions against me and on my parents who pressured me. Ultimately, it was my choice to follow through with the abortion. It wasn't until I came to grips with my responsibility for my abortion and confessed and repented of my sin that I experienced a life of freedom, walking in Christ's love, forgiveness, and healing.

The sin of abortion is a heavy burden to bear. Proverbs 18:14 says it plainly: "A man's spirit will endure sickness, but a crushed spirit who can bear?" It can be deeply painful to acknowledge the gravity of taking the life of your baby. Oftentimes, to sidestep the pain, women and men who have had an abortion will try to defend what they have done.

Perhaps you've seen photos online of pro-choice women wearing T-shirts that read "Shout your abortion!" Or maybe you've seen news coverage of pro-choice marches with women waving protest signs that read "My body. My choice." Social media feeds are filled with claims that women's reproductive "rights" are being taken away. Celebrity influencers share their abortion experiences with fans and tout them as being the best thing they ever did for their careers.

Yet consider for a moment that people who don't know Jesus don't know what to do with the guilt and shame they feel over their sins. They attempt to shrug it off. But it's not that simple. Sin sticks with us when it is not confessed and we don't repent, refusing to acknowledge it as offensive and heartbreaking to a holy God.

Some people try to rationalize their abortions by making excuses. They may say something like, "I was young and didn't know any better. I shouldn't be held accountable for a choice that I made so long ago." Or perhaps, they think, "I honestly didn't believe it was a baby. I thought that it was just a clump of cells or tissue." My excuse was the horrible state of mind I was in after losing Lauren. Though I never said it out loud, I thought, *If people knew what I have been through, they would understand.*

Blame shifting is another way we refuse to acknowledge our sin. As I stated earlier, I tried shifting all of the blame onto my parents. Adam and Eve also played the "blame game" after they had sinned against God. Eve blamed the serpent for her choice while Adam blamed both God and Eve for his choice (Genesis 3:8–13). Indeed, some women didn't have a say in their abortion (i.e., they were forced to have an abortion as a minor by their parents or coerced by threats of physical harm from an abusive partner). However, if you were capable of saying no to the pressure to abort, God wants you to humbly acknowledge your sin to him.

Maybe you are afraid that if you take responsibility for your abortion that it will let any other people who were involved off the hook—but they too are accountable before God for the role they played. Just remember that you can't place the blame for your decisions on other people. To experience the forgiveness, healing, and freedom God offers through Jesus, it is important to be honest before him and acknowledge your part in the abortion decision.

One additional way that a Christian may try to justify an abortion is by defaulting to God's grace. I too rationalized my abortion by taking advantage of God's grace and forgiveness. During the days leading up to my abortion, I kept trying to make deals with God to somehow excuse my abortion, and that my case should be an exception to the rule. With one last response, I remember praying, "God, I know that if this is truly wrong, you will forgive me." However, James 4:17 says, "So whoever knows the right thing to do and fails to do it, for him it is sin." I knew what I was doing was wrong. If you have taken advantage of God's grace to justify your abortion, you need to confess this as sin too and repent.

Whatever reason you have been using to justify your abortion, God wants you to confess your abortion to him as sin and repent so you can experience his healing. Proverbs 28:13 holds a stark warning to the unrepentant, but it also offers a beautiful promise to those who confess and repent instead of making excuses. It states, "People who conceal their sins will not prosper, but if they confess and turn from them, they will receive mercy" (NLT).

IDOLATRY AND ABORTION

Why am I discussing idolatry in a book about abortion? Because idolatry may be one of the culprits keeping you from moving forward after your abortion. Over the years, I have found that Christian women have often confessed and repented of the general act of abortion, but have never recognized the sin that motivated them to have an abortion in the first place—idolatry.

But what is an idol? Is it a carved statue that you worship? Not usually in our modern world. Instead, an idol is anything that you value and desire more than God. We are made to worship God. We flourish as humans only when we have God and his love at the center of our lives. But because of sin, we put other desires at the center of our lives. And in effect, we end up worshiping what we want instead of worshiping God. Yet idols never fully satisfy. Ultimately, if they are not identified and dealt with, they end up enslaving us in sin (2 Peter 2:19).

Idols can even be fashioned out of good things: a stellar marriage, an obedient child, a fun friendship, a safe home, a satisfying job, an excellent education, etc. But have some of these good things become your god? Has some person or thing become the top priority in your life, becoming your main focus? Has it taken God's place as the center of your worship? You can tell what you worship by evaluating what you spend your time, money, and affection on. We will often sacrifice to get what we want—or to keep it. You may be willing to sacrifice your sleep, health, financial stability, or even your relationships for what you have put at the center of your thoughts, hopes, dreams, and desires.

I'd like you to consider the correlation between what you worship and your abortion. At the heart of all abortion is a desire for something to happen—or not happen. What was at the heart of your desires surrounding your choice to abort your baby? If you have had multiple abortions, keep in mind that you may have had a different motive for each one. Let's look at a few scenarios to help you think about how worshiping anything besides God might motivate an abortion.

Scenario One:

A young couple met while attending a Christian university. As they began dating, they chose to become sexually active, which resulted in an unexpected pregnancy. Out of fear, they chose to have an abortion. What was the idol behind their fear? Could it have been fear of losing their reputation as "good" Christians? If they feared expulsion from school, could the idol have been their future careers and the possibility of not securing a good job after graduation, or having to start over at another school? Having a child would certainly make school harder, possibly take longer, and put a strain on finances. Did they sacrifice their baby's life because they didn't want to delay their four-year plan to graduate?

Scenario Two:

A youth pastor's unmarried teenage daughter became pregnant. He secretly took her to have an abortion. Was the youth pastor's idol his reputation at church and within the Christian community? Did he fear losing his ability to effectively teach the teens who looked up to him? Or was he afraid of losing his job and never being able to work in a church again? He sacrificed his grandchild's life to protect himself from any repercussions that his family might have to endure because of his daughter's choice to become sexually active.

Scenario Three:

An ob–gyn delivered some somber news to his once-excited patient and her husband. Recent scans had shown that their baby had some significant abnormalities. The doctor presented a bleak picture of the baby's health and what the couple's daily life might look like parenting a child with this condition. So, they had an abortion. Was money the idol as they worried about their financial stability if the medical bills and long-term health care costs started stacking up? Was health or life of ease an idol as they worried about having the physical, mental, and emotional stamina required to parent a child with special needs for the rest of their lives?

These are just a few scenarios to help you think through what motivated you to have an abortion. Fear is often the motivator in having an abortion, but selfishness can be too. A woman may not want to endure the physical change to her body. A man may not want to settle down and take care of a family, choosing instead to continue his carefree single lifestyle. Whatever the motive, idolatry is at the root of every abortion. The good news is that God is willing to forgive us regardless of which sinful motive precipitated our sinful action.

If you have only confessed to the act of abortion without considering your thoughts and desires leading up to your decision, then you may not have realized how important the motive of the heart is to God (1 Samuel 16:7). Many Christians have a wrong understanding of how God views our sin. He doesn't only call us to repent of the sinful actions we commit. God wants us to confess the sinful inclinations of the heart and mind as well. Isaiah 29:13 says, "These people say they are mine. They honor me with their lips, but their hearts are far from me. And their worship of me is nothing but man-made rules learned by rote" (NLT).

The good news is that Jesus died to atone for all manner of sin, including the sins of idolatry and abortion. You only need to come to him with a humble and repentant heart, confessing your sins to him (Romans 10:9–13). In doing so, you will find that Jesus is a forgiving Savior who is ready and willing to cleanse and heal you. In 1 John 1:9 God tells us, "If we confess our sins, he is faithful and just to forgive us our sins and to cleanse us from all unrighteousness." That is a promise.

If you don't come to God for forgiveness, you are keeping yourself cut off from all hope, help, and healing. The psalmist shares what would have happened if he had refused to confess his sin to the Lord. "If I had not confessed the sin in my heart, the Lord would not have listened" (Psalm 66:18 NLT).

But God is willing to listen when we confess. Consider the rest of what the psalmist wrote: "Come and listen, all you who fear God, and I will tell you what he did for me. For I cried out to him for help, praising him as I spoke. If I had not confessed the sin in my heart, the Lord would not have listened. But God did listen! He paid attention to my prayer. Praise God, who did not ignore my prayer or withdraw his unfailing love from me" (Psalm 66:16–20 NLT).

If your sin has caused you to feel distant from God, you do not have to feel far away from him any longer— no matter how long it's been since you've come to him. If you have never turned from your sins and come to Jesus, but you want to, simply confess that you are a sinner in need of a Savior. Today, right now as you are reading this, you can draw near to God through confession and repentance and he will draw near to you (James 4:8).

You can also pause now and take time to confess your abortion to God (each one that you have had) as well as the idolatry behind it. Examples of idols that you may have had at the time of your abortion are money, reputation, control, education, career, and relationships. God may bring other idols to your mind as you pray.

If you don't know what to pray, tell him that it was wrong to let the pressure of your circumstances and the desires of your heart dictate your decision to abort your baby. When you are finished confessing, thank him for listening to you and forgiving you of your abortion and the idols behind it. Then, like the psalmist, you can praise God that he has heard you and that he loves you with an unfailing love.

FOR REFLECTION

1. What measures have you taken to try to escape the unbearable weight of your abortion? In other words, have you refused to acknowledge it, tried to justify it, excuse it, or shift the blame to someone else? If so, how?

2. What hope does it give you to know that God is willing to listen to you when you confess your sin to him—including your abortion and idolatry?

Read through these passages and reflect on the benefits of confessing and repenting of your abortion and drawing near to God. Write out one or two truths and how you will apply them to your life.

- Psalm 32:1–5
- Psalm 73:28

FURTHER READING

- Camille Cates, *Pregnancy Crisis: This Wasn't the Plan* (Greensboro, NC: New Growth Press, 2023).
- Elyse M. Fitzpatrick, *Comforts from the Cross: Celebrating the Gospel One Day at a Time* (Wheaton, IL: Crossway, 2011).

- Elyse M. Fitzpatrick, *Idols of the Heart: Learning to Long for God Alone* (Phillipsburg, NJ: P&R Publishing, 2016).

Chapter 4

WILL I EVER STOP
FEELING THIS WAY?

Processing your thoughts and emotions after an abortion can be daunting. You may have felt like it's all too much to work through on your own. Yet, you may not have asked for help, believing no one could possibly understand what you've been through. Maybe you're scared to lift the lid off your heart, afraid of emotions boiling over and spilling out into your life, making things messy. However, God wants you to understand why you feel the way that you do, especially if it is hindering your relationship with him or other people.

READING YOUR EMOTIONS RIGHT

Emotions were given to us by God to indicate that something deeper is going on inside of us. They also motivate us to take action. This can be good as long as we are reading them right. I've heard that emotions can be compared to the various lights on a car dashboard. When one of these signals lights up, such as "check engine," "battery alert," or "seat belt reminder," it means that something is wrong with the car and needs attention. If you ignore the signal, it doesn't mean that the problem is going away. In fact, it often gets worse over time.

So it is with our emotions. They indicate that something within us needs attention. Whatever is bothering us will not go away until we tend to it. The problem is that many of us treat our hearts and minds like we do the car dashboard lights. We choose to ignore the warning signals, and we end up getting worse.

While a car manual will tell you what each warning light means, you must take the car to a trained mechanic to fix it. Likewise, it makes sense to take your heart to the Lord for him to explain what's going on when your emotions are wreaking havoc in your life.

WHY IS THE CHECK ENGINE LIGHT ON?

Part of the problem with abortion is what it does to a woman physically. God created women's bodies to uniquely protect and nurture preborn babies as well as give birth to them. He designed a mother's womb to be the place where he knits and weaves together a new little life.

Inside the womb, God fearfully and wonderfully works the strands of a father's and mother's DNA together to form and shape their baby (Psalm 139:13–16). Psalm 139:15 states, "My frame was not hidden from you, when I was being made in secret." This language paints the picture of God's intentions for the womb to be a safe place—secret and hidden away from external dangers that could harm the baby whom he has made in his image (Genesis 1:27). It's his way of providing loving protection for the most vulnerable and helpless human beings. The Hebrew word *cether*, translated "secret" in Psalm 139:15, is used throughout the Psalms to describe a place of safety and refuge in times of danger or threat of danger (Psalm 27:5, 31:20, 32:7, 61:4, 91:1, 119:114).

An elective abortion is an unnatural act upon a woman's body and goes against her God-given instincts to protect and nurture her baby. So of course the physical and mental damage done by the procedure affects her. Therefore, an abortion tends to stir a woman's emotions, which can be extremely difficult for her to process on her own.

Men are also affected by abortion and may also exhibit strong emotions afterward. God intended for a man to want to shield and shelter from harm the child he has fathered. A mother and father's natural inclinations are to safeguard the baby developing in her womb.

As the result of an abortion, the "check engine" light of your heart may have been going off for quite some time. The Bible not only talks about emotions, but it directs us to Our Maker to fix what is setting them off. With this in mind, it is best to look at what the Bible says about dealing with any emotions you have experienced in relation to your abortion. We can't explore every emotion in depth. But, I will touch on some of the most common emotions a woman encounters after an abortion.

RESPONDING TO GUILT AND GRIEF

Part of the emotional pain a woman feels after her abortion is due to guilt and grief. Whether you believed abortion was right or wrong at the time, the Bible says that your conscience convicts you of sin. Consider Romans 2:15 which says, "[People] show that the work of the law is written on their hearts, while their conscience also bears witness, and their conflicting thoughts accuse or even excuse them." God's law is written on your heart, even if you denied that your abortion was wrong at the time. Your conscience bears witness to your sin and it weighs heavily on you.

As to grief, if you acknowledge that your abortion was sin, you may be grieving that you sinned against God and your baby. You may also be grieving over the loss of your baby. For some women, that grief doesn't surface until they desire to start having children or become pregnant again.

While guilt and grief are prominent emotions a woman experiences after an abortion, other feelings can bubble to the surface, making it confusing to get to the root of your guilt and grief. Exploring the emotions that have surfaced can help you finally deal with the deeper emotions of guilt and grief.

EXAMINING ANGER

Would people describe you as an angry person? Could the underlying cause of your anger be your abortion? It's important to understand that anger can be righteous or unrighteous. Some people believe that we rarely experience righteous anger. That simply is not true. God has righteous anger over sin (Psalm 7:11). Therefore, since we are made in his image, we can (and should) also experience righteous anger over sin (Ephesians

4:26). Because we live in a sinful, fallen world, we witness sin's destructive effects, and it makes us angry. However, we often express our anger—righteous as well as unrighteous—by sinning against God and other people. We tend to vent our anger and take it out on others instead of responding thoughtfully, slowly, and righteously (James 1:19–20).

Most likely, there are people who have sinned against you in relation to your abortion. Is it your husband or boyfriend who pushed for the abortion? Perhaps it is a friend who suggested abortion as a solution to your unexpected pregnancy. Is it the nurse at the abortion clinic who treated you coldly? Maybe it is the doctor who received payment to perform your abortion. Whatever it is, their sin against God and against you has made you righteously angry. Take some time to talk to God about your righteous anger over the suffering and heartache their sin has caused you.

Of course, it is important to recognize that you may also be experiencing unrighteous anger. This type of anger is centered around self instead of sin. It often comes from a desire to defend yourself or retaliate against others. You may have been angry at a friend who tried to talk you out of the abortion—anticipating an "I told you so," instead of admitting that she was right in what she said. Or your anger might stem from thinking your abortion was going to help you hold onto a relationship with the baby's father. As is common, the abortion may have actually distanced the two of you and resulted in a breakup. These are just a couple of examples of unrighteous anger.

For me, I was angry with my boyfriend who had taken Lauren's life. I often thought, "I wouldn't even be in this position if it wasn't for you." The truth was, I didn't have to have an abortion. That was my own choice. I couldn't shift the blame to him completely. I also needed to take responsibility. I was righteously angry over his sin against me and Lauren. But, I was unrighteously angry at him for the abortion even though I was the one who chose to go through with it.

As people who experience sin and suffering in this world, sometimes we feel anger toward God. But be careful of how you handle your anger. Remember that God has not sinned against you.

Our limited understanding of suffering can cause us frustration that we direct at God. Instead, he invites us to pour out our hurts and frustration to him, lamenting our struggles to him, and seeking his help. If you have been angry with God about your pregnancy and the events leading up to your abortion, you can express your hurt and confusion to him for he cares for you (Psalm 142:1–2). Then, confess your sin of anger against him and seek his forgiveness for leaning on your own understanding rather than trusting his plan for you and your baby (Proverbs 3:5–6).

Refuse to keep holding God at arms' length out of anger. He is the only one who can comfort and heal you. He loves you and has a plan for your life. Take your angry feelings to him and let him help you work through them.

As you can see, feelings of anger after an abortion can be very complex. When there are several people involved in an abortion decision (and there usually are) it can be difficult to sort out who was responsible for what. It is important for you to take personal responsibility for your part in the abortion while also addressing the sin of others against you. It helps to sort out who you are angry with and why. Make a list of people you are angry with regarding your abortion and why. Then ask God to help you think through whether each instance should be considered righteous anger or unrighteous anger.

This will serve you well when you learn about forgiving the other people involved in your abortion in chapter 6. If you have not acknowledged being sinned against, you will probably find yourself stuck in anger (and conflict). Ask God to help you resolve your righteous anger toward them so that you can live at peace (Romans 12:17–18). This will take much effort and time, but it is part of God's healing and sanctifying work in the hearts of those who belong to him.

OVERCOMING ANXIETY

The shame a woman feels after an abortion often leads to the fear of other people finding out about it. If she has had multiple abortions, the shame tends to pile on top of shame, compounding her fears. And that fear can fester into anxiety. Proverbs 12:25 says, "Anxiety in a man's heart weighs him down, but a good word makes him glad." Anxiety over your abortion is a heavy thing to carry around for the rest of your life. But Scripture says that you don't have to be burdened with anxiety. First Peter 5:7 instructs you to cast "all your anxieties on [Jesus], because he cares for you"—not some of your anxieties, but all of them, including anxiety over people finding out about your abortion.

But perhaps you are in the same position I was after my abortion. As a Christian, I already knew that Jesus forgave me for my abortion. However, I had not understood that biblical healing was available to me as well (i.e., working through my emotions and experiences according to God's Word, uncovering the idolatry behind my abortion, confessing and repenting of my sin, receiving God's forgiveness and extending forgiveness to others).

Do you want to know what God's greatest means of healing is? Psalm 107:20 says, "He sent out his word and healed them, and delivered them from their destruction." It wasn't until I opened the Bible and began to apply it to my life that I started to heal. Dealing with my idolatry surrounding my abortion—something I didn't even know that I needed to do—and confessing the motive of my heart as sin to the Lord brought such restoration as I drew near to him instead of being distant from him for several years. Addressing the guilt and shame I felt by being able to openly acknowledge my part in the abortion—as well as being able to voice the incredible hurt caused by my boyfriend, my parents, and the abortion clinic staff—brought such cleansing and comfort as I received God's grace in place of the guilt and shame. Once this sanctification and healing began, it freed me from the anxiety of other people finding out about my abortion, and I was finally no longer living under the shadow of shame.

What about your self-inflicted wounds—the mental and emotional pain your own sin has caused you? Is God willing to heal those as well? Yes! It's in his nature. In Exodus 15:26, God says of himself "I am the Lord, your healer." If you haven't already, come to Jesus as your Healer. Ask him to heal your heart, to bind up the self-inflicted wounds of your sin. Pause now and pray Psalm 41:4 out loud to him: "O Lord, be gracious to me; heal me, for I have sinned against you!" God promises to be near those who have humble hearts, to save them, and heal them (Psalm 34:18, 147:3).

DEALING WITH DEPRESSION

If your abortion is causing you to despair of hope, or of life itself, it is important to work through what is causing your depression. Christians can be overwhelmed by deep feelings of sadness, not knowing why they feel so grieved or distant from God. Many of the psalms give voice to the depression we feel. Psalm 42 is a particularly rich passage to work through. Twice, the psalmist asks this question of his own soul: "Why are you cast down, O my soul, and why are you in turmoil within me?" (vv. 5, 11).

The depression, despair, or even dread you are sensing might point to one of two things: you may have unconfessed sin over something related to your abortion and it has you feeling heavyhearted, or grief has a firm grip on your heart—perhaps both. Let's focus on the possibility of unconfessed sin for a moment. Psalm 32:1–5 helps us to understand the stress and strain of unconfessed sin as well as the delight of confessing it to the Lord. It says:

Blessed is the one whose transgression is forgiven,
   whose sin is covered.
Blessed is the man against whom the Lord counts
   no iniquity,
      and in whose spirit there is no deceit.

For when I kept silent, my bones wasted away
   through my groaning all day long.
For day and night your hand was heavy upon me;
   my strength was dried up as by the heat of
      summer.   *Selah*

I acknowledged my sin to you,
   and I did not cover my iniquity;
I said, "I will confess my transgressions to the
   Lord,"
      and you forgave the iniquity of my sin. *Selah*

Maybe you've racked your brain to think of any unconfessed sin and nothing comes to mind. In Psalm 139, David cries out, "Search me, O God, and know my heart! Try me and know my thoughts! And see if there be any grievous way in me, and lead me in the way everlasting!" (vv. 23–24). Pause now and use this passage as a prayer to the Lord, asking him to reveal any sin that you may not be seeing. When we humble ourselves before him, he is faithful to kindly convict us of any sin that needs to be confessed.

If no sin stands out to you, then consider that the root of your depression or prolonged sadness might be that you are stuck in grief. We will explore what the Bible says about grief in the next chapter.

WHAT IF I'M JUST NUMB?

While the physical pain from an abortion eventually subsides, the emotional pain continues for months, years, or even decades afterward. By nature, what do we tend to do when we are experiencing pain? We try to get rid of it! If we can't remove whatever is causing us pain, we'll seek to numb ourselves from the pain. It might seem like it's better to be numb than to feel pain, but the danger in becoming numb is that we stop feeling anything at all.

Prolonged emotional numbness causes your heart to become dull or calloused, even cynical. Jesus speaks of those who have allowed their hearts to grow dull. He likens such dullness to the impairment of our hearing and sight, which then affects our being able to recognize our need for him (Matthew 13:13–17). Consider verse 15, which says, "For this people's heart has grown dull, and with their ears they can barely hear, and their eyes they have closed, lest they should see with their eyes and hear with their ears and understand with their heart and turn, and I would heal them."

When you have sinned, or been sinned against, and suffered for it, instead of growing calloused and becoming numb, you must turn to Jesus. His Word offers you hope and help in addressing the emotional pain from your abortion experience. Most of all, he wants to heal you.

If you are struggling with a heart and mind that have grown numb or calloused to the sin of your abortion, ask God to give you eyes to see your sin in light of his holiness. You can pray this prayer:

Jesus, help me to see the depths of my sin in comparison to your holiness—your goodness and purity. Help me to see that my sin of abortion destroyed my child whom you created for your glory and purpose. I confess my abortion (each one) as sin against you and against my baby. I repent and look to you for help and healing. I know that as I look to you for help, I "will be radiant with joy and no shadow of shame will darken [my] face" (Psalm 34:5 NLT).

As you allow yourself to feel remorse for your sin, it prompts you to seek and receive God's forgiveness. He is loving, gracious, and merciful. Because of his sacrifice on the cross, Jesus stands ready to forgive sin and bring healing through his work of sanctification. This, in turn, brings freedom and joy as you walk with him and move beyond your abortion experience.

FOR REFLECTION

1. What emotions have you been experiencing since your abortion?

2. For each emotion that you mentioned above, write out any thoughts or beliefs that have been a driving force behind that emotion.

3. Have you felt completely numb since your abortion? After reading this chapter, why do you think you have felt numb?

Read through these passages and reflect on the removal of guilt and shame, working through anger, anxiety, and depression. Write out one or two truths and how you will apply them to your life. You can also use these passages as prayers to God.

- Psalm 25:1–12
- James 1:19–21
- Psalm 142:1–5

FURTHER READING

- Robert D. Jones, *Angry at God? Bring Him Your Doubt and Questions* (Phillipsburg, NJ: P&R Publishing, 2003).
- Timothy S. Lane, *Freedom from Guilt: Finding Release from Your Burdens* (Greensboro, NC: New Growth Press, 2020).
- Edward T. Welch, *Depression: The Way Up When You're Feeling Down* (Greensboro, NC: New Growth Press, 2011).
- Edward T. Welch. *When I Am Afraid: A Step-by-Step Guide Away from Fear and Anxiety* (Greensboro, NC: New Growth Press, 2008).

Chapter 5

WHAT DO I DO
WITH THESE THOUGHTS
ABOUT THE BABY?

The human mind has trouble processing death and trauma. I believe that is because our hearts hold the echo of Eden. Deep down we know death and trauma are bad, the result of living in a broken world. So even if we never verbally express our thoughts about the tragic impact abortion has on us, it still takes its toll on the mind. It's not uncommon for a woman who has had an abortion to suffer nightmares, day terrors, or recurring daydreams about her baby. It's the mind's way of trying to process all that she has experienced in the loss of her child.

While it is good and right to think about your aborted baby, it is unhelpful to be retraumatized again and again through painful, and sometimes horrifying, dreams or thoughts. God wants us to have sound minds and hearts that are at peace after we have confessed the sin of abortion to him. Isaiah 26:3 tells us, "You keep him in perfect peace whose mind is [fixed] on you, because he trusts in you." As you look to Jesus, it will help you to both acknowledge that your baby was a person to whom God gave life and then grieve the death and loss of your baby.

YOU LOST *YOUR* BABY

I remember counseling a Christian woman who had had an abortion with her husband while they were still dating in college. Neither one of them was a Christian at the time. Even after they became Christians, they had never discussed their abortion. When I shared with her at church one day about my abortion, she said, "You know, I thought I had dealt with my abortion, but in talking to you about it, I find myself tearing up even now. I'm not sure I have really worked through what happened."

As she and I walked through a Bible study together, God did an incredible work of cleansing and healing in her heart. During one of our weekly meetings, she told me, "Anytime I have ever thought of or spoken about my abortion, I never put a possessive pronoun in front of the word 'baby.' I've only referred to what happened as 'the abortion' or 'the baby I aborted.' But that was *my* baby. God has worked in my heart to acknowledge my baby's life. It was *my* baby that I aborted."

Many women still believe the falsehood that it's not a baby being aborted, but merely a clump of cells, or cluster of tissue, especially if the abortion occurred early on in the pregnancy. Our world doesn't want to acknowledge the personhood of aborted babies. The pro-choice narrative uses words like *embryo* or *fetus*, and rarely, if ever, uses the word *baby*. And yet, we know it's a baby. Women who are excited about their pregnancies proudly post ultrasound pics on their social media pages. Yet, the babies being proudly featured by mom and dad are often at the same gestational age as aborted babies. The only difference behind the terminology being used—"here's the ultrasound of my baby" versus "the pill she took aborted the embryo"—is the desire of the mother or father's heart.

When I was given an ultrasound at the abortion clinic, I looked away because I didn't want to see my baby fluttering and moving around on the screen. To do so would have been an acknowledgment of his little life. It would have made it that much harder for me to be calloused and follow through with the abortion.

So, when God begins to work in a woman's heart, bringing conviction that she aborted *her* baby, she often feels the need to do something to acknowledge her baby's personhood. The woman I counseled did so by verbalizing that it was her baby. She then stated, "I don't have two children, but three." The deep sense of joy she experienced in recognizing and honoring all of her children was apparent. What freedom comes to the woman who is finally willing and able to affirm this truth!

TAKING TIME TO GRIEVE YOUR BABY

Along with this acknowledgment can come significant grief. Oftentimes, a woman who has had an abortion has never grieved the loss of her baby. Sometimes a woman doesn't believe she has a right to grieve since she was the one who ended her baby's life. Yet, anytime we have lost someone, we can and should grieve. Have you grieved over the death of your baby? Grief is one way that God helps mothers and fathers to process the thoughts and feelings they wrestle with after their abortions.

Let's consider how people in Scripture grieved when someone died. They often followed the popular mourning practices of their time, such as rending (i.e., tearing) their clothes, wearing sackcloth, and putting ashes on their heads (Genesis 37:34, Joel 1:8). Frequently, people would come to the house of the person who had died and wail loudly or play music (Jeremiah 9:17–18, Matthew 9:23). These examples may seem odd in contemporary Western culture, but these people were demonstrating outwardly the grief they were experiencing inwardly.

In modern times, we often try to hide our grief and pain instead of showing it. As we've seen, in biblical times, they were unafraid to express it. Jesus did not hide his grief when his friend Lazarus died. Jesus openly wept even though he knew he was about to raise Lazarus from the dead (John 11:35).

Death stings. In mourning the loss of your baby, you can voice your grief to the Lord. Perhaps it would even help to share your sorrows with a trusted friend. Don't hide it or suppress it. If you have been doing so, this is likely the cause of any nightmares, day terrors, or recurring daydreams you are having.

If you have had multiple abortions, it could be that you have only grieved over your abortion as a singular event. It is essential that you acknowledge each life and grieve the death of each of your babies. They are unique individuals, every single one an image-bearer of God whom he formed in your womb.

It is important to note that people experience grief differently. Also, grief is not a one-and-done event. While there is no specific mourning period set in the Bible, the outward, public demonstration eventually did end. It must. We are meant to live life, not be swallowed up in mourning the death of our loved ones. At the same time, personal grieving ebbs and flows and never ends this side of heaven. When the tidal waves of grief hit, continue to pour out your thoughts and feelings to the Lord as well as to a trusted friend who will listen patiently and pray with you.

WHERE IS MY BABY NOW?

Something that can keep a woman who has had an abortion stuck in her grief is wondering what happened to her baby—both body and soul—after the abortion. Several years after my abortion, and many years after I went through the Bible study that started my healing process, out of the blue I was stricken with the thought of what happened to my baby's body after the abortion. I don't recall signing any paperwork or saying something designating my wishes.

I can only assume my baby's body was treated as waste or biohazard material. A tsunami of grief hit me afresh! I cried and cried. I grieved deeply before the Lord and mourned the fact that instead of my baby being placed in the arms of a loving adoptive couple, my baby's little body was most likely discarded like trash.

Anger welled up in me anew—righteous anger at the abortion clinic staff, nurses, and doctors. But because I had learned how to biblically process my anger and other emotions, I was able to pour out my heart to the Lord, choose to forgive, and walk in peace again.

Of course, it also helped me to know that baby's soul was in heaven, under the loving care of my Savior. As you have grieved over your abortion and mourned the loss of your baby, perhaps you have also wondered about your baby's eternal destiny. While God's Word does not have explicit details about what happens to children's souls after they die, there is some encouragement to be found in the account of the death of King David's baby.

After David's baby dies, he finalizes his mourning and says something quite interesting. In 2 Samuel 12:23 he states, "But now he is dead. Why should I fast? Can I bring him back again? I shall go to him, but he will not return to me." David was known as a man after God's heart (Acts 13:22). So, we can reasonably presume that David was going to be with God in heaven after he died. According to the statement "I shall go to him," David seems to believe that he is going to see his baby again in heaven.

Though we will always grieve the loss of our loved ones in this life on earth, Christians can and should grieve differently. We grieve as those who have hope in Jesus, our resurrected Savior (1 Thessalonians 4:13). One day, he will resurrect his people and we will spend eternity with him. And death? It will be no more. According to Revelation 21:4, Christ will "wipe away every tear from their eyes, and death shall be no more, neither shall there be mourning, nor crying, nor pain anymore, for the former things have passed away." Won't that be a glorious day?

SHOULD I NAME MY BABY?

Well-meaning Christians, counselors, and abortion trauma ministries have often encouraged women to name their aborted children and have a memorial for them as part of the grieving process. But nowhere does the Bible indicate that a woman has not properly grieved and healed until she has done these things.

In fact, in the story of King David's baby who died, there is no example of doing either of these things. David's baby dies, he comforts his wife after the loss of their son, and that is all we know from Scripture (2 Samuel 12:24). At the same time, there is nothing in the Bible instructing you to refrain from naming your aborted baby if you want to.

My husband, who was not my aborted baby's father, wanted to acknowledge the personhood of my baby by naming him. So, together we prayed and decided on a name. Later, when I told my other children (who were in their teens at the time) about their aborted sibling, my oldest daughter asked if the baby had a middle name. When I told her no, she asked if they could give him one. This was such a precious time for our family as ordained by God's providence.

The point is that no one should tell you that you haven't grieved over the loss of your baby or "properly" healed if you haven't named your baby. In fact, many women don't know if their baby was a boy or a girl because the abortion occurred too early in the pregnancy, or they were not/did not want to be informed of the baby's gender. The only thing necessary for true healing after abortion is drawing near to God through his Word. In doing so, you will find his love, forgiveness, cleansing, grace, and mercy to move forward.

SHOULD I HAVE A MEMORIAL FOR MY BABY?

As far as having a memorial for your baby, that can be a good thing to do as long as it honors the Lord's gift of life and your baby's personhood. However, I would caution you not to let your baby's memorial become some sort of a shrine. Over the years, I've known many grieving parents who stayed stuck in their grief. Oftentimes, they would create elaborate memorials for the children they lost. And they would visit that place of mourning very often, sometimes daily. Or they might stay there for hours on end.

Any memorial you choose to do or make for your baby should express godly sorrow over your loss and be a celebration of their existence. When I was finally able to talk openly about my aborted baby without fear of condemnation, I wanted a piece of jewelry made with all of my children's names on it. I don't wear it daily, but it is precious to me and I wear it often.

We also have Christmas ornaments for each of our children. I even have ones that I received for my daughter Lauren's first Christmas. It hangs on the tree every year. But my aborted baby didn't have one for a long time. That bothered my oldest daughter. She wanted all of her siblings to be represented on the family tree. It was her way of acknowledging his life and membership in our family. It now hangs on our Christmas tree each year. If you would like to do something in memory of your baby, find something that honors the Lord and is meaningful to you.

FOR REFLECTION

1. In what ways did you deny the personhood of your baby at the time of your abortion?

2. How can you acknowledge his or her life now?

3. Have you ever grieved over the loss of your baby? If not, why do you think that is? If you have grieved, what did that time of grieving look like?

4. Have you been stuck in your grief? If so, how can you begin to move forward with the Lord?

Read through these passages and reflect on what God's Word says about grief as well as our eternal hope. Write out one or two truths and how you will apply them to your life. Consider also writing a prayer to the Lord, expressing your grief to the Lord over the loss of your little one while acknowledging your baby's life as a gift from God.

- Psalm 62:5–8
- Isaiah 35:10
- Revelation 21:1–5

FURTHER READING

- Robert W. Kellemen, *God's Healing for Life's Losses: How to Find Hope When You're Hurting* (Winona Lake, IN: BMH Books, 2010).
- Paul Tautges, *A Small Book for the Hurting Heart: Meditations on Loss, Grief, and Healing* (Greensboro, NC: New Growth Press, 2020).

Chapter 6

WHY AM I STRUGGLING WITH FORGIVENESS?

It is in our nature to want to appear good. I would even argue that as God's image-bearers, some part of us knows that we should do good. When you have sinned, it can be tempting to try to do good works to make up for your sins. Sometimes, a woman who has had an abortion may volunteer at a Pregnancy Resource Center, share pro-life social media posts, or seek to minister to other women who have had an abortion.

These can all be good things to do. But, if your deepest motive is to do enough good things to compensate for your abortion, you will never reach your goal. Romans 3:10 says, "None is righteous, no, not one." You cannot earn God's forgiveness or favor by trying to offset your abortion with good deeds.

THE SORROW OF BETRAYAL

If you are having trouble believing that you are truly forgiven because you are filled with remorse, the Word of God tells us how best to deal with it. Psalm 51:17

proclaims, "The sacrifices of God are a broken spirit; a broken and contrite heart, O God, you will not despise." The Hebrew word for *contrite* in this verse is *daḳah* and it implies a humbly broken heart over sin.

Scripture provides examples of two of Jesus's followers who utterly betrayed him. However, their responses afterward were quite different. One turned inward, focusing on himself, and succumbed to self-hatred and self-destruction. The other turned outward, chose to focus on Jesus, and lived in the love of his Savior.

On the night of Christ's arrest, Judas Iscariot handed Jesus over to his enemies for thirty pieces of silver (Matthew 26:15). Judas loved money and financial gain more than he loved the Lord (John 12:1–6). As one of the twelve disciples, Judas was close to Jesus. Even though he knew Judas would betray him, Jesus loved Judas and allowed him to be part of his innermost circle. Jesus treated Judas with the same kindness as he did the rest of the disciples (John 13:1–30).

One of the most punch-in-the-gut scenes in the Bible is when Judas comes to Jesus in the garden of Gethsemane with a troop of Roman soldiers and Temple guards to arrest him (John 18:3). Judas greets Jesus with a kiss on the cheek as customary in those times, signifying whom they should arrest (Matthew 26:48–49). After receiving Judas's greeting, Jesus says to him, "Friend, do what you came to do" (Matthew 26:50). Jesus called Judas his friend, and he meant it. Psalm 41:9 speaks prophetically of this very moment: "Even my close friend in whom I trusted, who ate my bread, has lifted his heel against me."

After Jesus's arrest, Judas is burdened by the guilt and shame of his betrayal. Matthew 27:3–5 recounts the betrayer's response. It says, "Then when Judas, his betrayer, saw that Jesus was condemned, he changed his mind and brought back the thirty pieces of silver to the chief priests and the elders, saying, 'I have sinned by betraying innocent blood.' They said, 'What is that to us? See to it yourself.' And throwing down the pieces of silver into the temple, [Judas] departed, and he went and hanged himself." Instead of turning to the Giver of Life to receive forgiveness, Judas takes his own life.

Another one of Jesus's disciples, Simon Peter, had boasted that he would never abandon the Lord (Matthew 26:33–35). Yet, after Jesus's arrest, Peter shows his duplicity as he refuses to acknowledge any affiliation with Christ. Peter denies Jesus, not once, but three times (Matthew 26:69–74). Matthew 26:75 details the moment Peter is convicted of his sin and filled with immense regret over his own betrayal as it states, "And Peter remembered the saying of Jesus, 'Before the rooster crows, you will deny me three times.' And he went out and wept bitterly."

Both Judas and Peter demonstrate deep remorse over their sin against Jesus. However, their responses after they had sinned are vastly different. Judas expresses worldly sorrow, a sorrow filled with despair instead of hope (2 Corinthians 7:10). Judas is unwilling to turn to Jesus, receive forgiveness, and continue following him. The unrepentant disciple then takes drastic measures and ends his life still covered in guilt and shame. Judas makes his choice, and so does Peter.

Peter demonstrates godly sorrow and repentance when he encounters the risen Christ. When Peter sees Jesus, he moves toward the Lord, not away from him (John 21:1–19). This shows Peter's desire for restoration. And that's exactly what Jesus does. He restores him to ministry. Three times, once for each time Peter denied him, Jesus asks, "Do you love me?" (John 21:15–17). Peter responds every time with "You know that I love you." Jesus then reaffirms Peter by instructing him to care for other Christians just as a shepherd loves and cares for his sheep. Then he calls Peter to follow him once again (John 21:19). Peter does so with renewed fervor. He lives the remainder of his life boldly preaching the gospel of Jesus even in the face of persecution (Acts 2:14–39, 3:11–4:4, 4:8–12, 5:29–32, 10:34–43).

As you reflect on Judas's betrayal and Peter's betrayal, you may want to note that each of the twelve disciples betrayed Jesus during his arrest and trial. And every single one of them had sworn that they would never betray him, but they all did (Matthew 26:35, 56). Followers of Christ can and still do sin—but God's grace is always sufficient to cover their sin.

THE FORGIVENESS OF CHRIST

Do you worry that Jesus's sacrificial work on the cross only covers certain sins? Maybe you believe that God forgives other people, but you don't see how God could ever forgive you for taking the life of your baby. Consider for a moment Jesus's declaration about himself when he says, "The Son of Man came to seek and to save the lost" (Luke 19:10).

Jesus shed his blood to provide atonement for people who are lost in their sin. Ephesians 1:7 says, "In him we have redemption through his blood, the forgiveness of our trespasses, according to the riches of his grace, which he lavished upon us, in all wisdom and insight." Scripture says that Jesus delights in lavishing the riches of his grace on undeserving sinners! The only thing you need to do to receive this lavish gift is to put your faith in him as your loving Lord and Savior.

Jesus took your sin upon himself, removed it from your record, and replaced it with his righteousness (2 Corinthians 5:21). In Hebrews 9:26, we find these compelling words: "He has appeared once for all . . . to put away sin by the sacrifice of himself." That wording, "put away," means to "abolish," or "thwart the efficacy of" sin. If you have put your faith in Jesus, he has done away with your sin of abortion. On the cross, Jesus abolished your abortion.

Have you placed your faith in Jesus to cover all your sins, including abortion? If so, God promises freedom for those who come to him: "For freedom Christ has set us free" (Galatians 5:1). Does this sound like God wants you to remain stuck in your past, living under the burden of sin? He wants you to live in the freedom Jesus has purchased for you.

THE LIE OF SELF-FORGIVENESS

In my years as a counselor, I have learned that the single biggest factor keeping women from receiving God's forgiveness and walking in freedom is the belief that they need to forgive themselves. Regarding your abortion, perhaps you too have thought, *God might forgive me, but I can never forgive myself.* The lie of self-forgiveness has been reinforced via Christian-themed books, songs, and movies and has even been taught by some Christian leaders. But self-forgiveness is not a biblical concept and undermines the forgiveness that can only be found in Christ.

God's Word teaches that we must accept the blood atonement of Christ as sufficient for the forgiveness of sin. The forgiveness of sin only comes from redemption in Christ through his blood (Hebrews 9:15, 22). You cannot redeem yourself. You cannot atone for your own sin. Therefore, you cannot forgive yourself. Will you refuse to believe the lie of self-forgiveness and accept the free and full forgiveness that Christ has already bought with his blood on your behalf?

THE BEAUTY OF FORGIVENESS

Accepting God's free and full forgiveness also helps you to forgive those who have sinned against you. In Matthew 18:21–35, Jesus tells the parable of the unmerciful servant. This is a great passage to work through if you seem stuck in unforgiveness and remain resentful toward someone over your abortion. Pausing right now to read through this passage may help you to reexamine your heart for any unresolved anger preventing you from being willing to forgive. If you are still seething in anger, go back to your list from chapter 4 to work through who you are angry with and why. Remember to identify whether your anger is righteous or unrighteous.

Then, take time to deal with each person you are angry with according to God's Word. In Ephesians 4:31, we are commanded to "Let all bitterness and wrath and anger and clamor and slander be put away from you, along with all malice." In obedience to Jesus, we must "put away" from us all bitterness, wrath, anger, clamor, slander, and malice. In the original Greek wording, the idea is to remove anger from your heart, not just to stop being angry.[1] It implies intentionally removing it and putting it away from you—your thoughts, feelings, and actions.

Once anger is removed, you must replace it with something good, or you will be tempted to let anger creep back in again. Ephesians 4:32 offers the appropriate replacements of "[being] kind to one another, tenderhearted, forgiving one another, as God in Christ forgave you." So, don't just seek to remove anger from your heart, replace it with kindness, tenderheartedness, and forgiveness.

Some Christians think that forgiveness is a process, that it takes time, and that you can't truly forgive someone until you feel like forgiving them. But that's not what God's Word teaches. Reflecting on Ephesians 4:32, you see that God commands kindness, tenderheartedness, and forgiveness. It is your choice to be obedient to do these things—not an easy choice, but God will help you to do it if you ask him. As you meditate on God's incredible kindness and compassion toward you, you will be enabled to extend compassion, kindness, and forgiveness toward other sinners.

As you have reflected on your abortion experience, most likely you discovered that you also have sinned against someone. You must seek forgiveness from those whom you have sinned against. Reflect on Matthew 5:23–24 which says, "So if you are offering your gift at the altar and there remember that your brother has something against you, leave your gift there before the altar and go. First be reconciled to your brother, and then come and offer your gift."

You cannot wholeheartedly worship God if you have not sought forgiveness from those you have sinned against (John 4:24, Romans 12:18). If you are concerned that in the other person's anger, they may do harm to you, you could send them written communication asking them to forgive you.

REACHING RECONCILIATION

Before we finish our discussion of forgiveness, it is important to clarify the difference between forgiveness and reconciliation. *Forgiveness* means choosing to no longer hold someone's wrongdoing against them. *Reconciliation* means mutually pursuing a restored relationship after it has been damaged by sin. A wise person once said, "It only takes one person to forgive, but it takes two to reconcile." There is a distinction between choosing to forgive someone from your heart who has not confessed and repented of their sin and choosing to reconcile with someone who has confessed and repented of their sin (Luke 17:3–4).

When two people humble themselves and confess and repent of their sins toward each other, reconciliation takes place. For example, if my husband and I both said something unkind to each other in the heat of conflict, I need to confess my sin to him and seek his forgiveness and he needs to confess his sin to me and seek my forgiveness. When forgiveness is requested and granted by both of us, reconciliation occurs.

It is possible that only one person was sinned against. So, if I sin against my husband by saying something unkind in a conflict, but he did not retaliate, I would be the only person who needs to confess and repent of sin. If I do so, and he extends his forgiveness to me, we are reconciled.

A relationship is never genuinely restored without reconciliation. Not only is it impossible to reconcile with someone until they are repentant, but it can be unwise and unsafe for you to try to reconcile with them, especially if they have previously been violent toward you. However, this should not hinder your obedience to the Lord in forgiving them from your heart.

I hope that you have come to understand the importance of forgiveness, both receiving God's forgiveness and extending forgiveness to others. I also pray that you refuse to believe the lie that you need to forgive yourself for your abortion. If you keep listening to that lie, it will hold you back from moving forward. In the next chapter, you will examine other things that may hinder your spiritual growth so that you can address them and press on in your walk with Jesus.

FOR REFLECTION

1. What, if anything, still holds you back from receiving God's forgiveness? What about extending forgiveness to others?

2. Why is God's forgiveness of your abortion such a wonderful thing?

Read through these passages to reflect on living in God's forgiveness as well as extending it to others. Write out one or two truths and how you will apply them to your life.

- Matthew 6:14–15
- Luke 6:37–38

FURTHER READING

- Timothy S. Lane, *Forgiving Others: Joining Wisdom and Love* (Greensboro, NC: New Growth Press, 2005).
- C. John Miller, *Accepting God's Forgiveness: Believing in God's Love for You* (Greensboro, NC: New Growth Press, 2011).

Chapter 7

HOW DO I LEAVE MY ABORTION IN THE PAST?

When considering your life's journey, I don't know if you can truly leave your abortion in the past. Every experience you go through becomes part of your larger story. With this in mind, *how* you view your abortion at this point in your life is what is most important. Do you still feel shame and condemnation, or are you living in the light of Christ's redemption? Are you moving forward and finding your comfort in God and his Word?

The book of Ecclesiastes talks about seasons. It says, "For everything there is a season, and a time for every matter under heaven" (Ecclesiastes 3:1). In verse four, it speaks about a time for sorrow and mourning over loss. But it also says there is a time to live in joy and celebrate. For the woman who has had an abortion, there is a time to weep and a time to mourn and also a time to laugh and a time to dance (Ecclesiastes 3:4). If God has healed you from the pain of your abortion, now is the time to laugh and dance.

You can, and should, rejoice over God's mercy and grace, his love, and his healing. If Jesus has set you free, there is no longer any condemnation from the past—only spiritual liberation in Christ to enjoy (Romans 8:1–2, Galatians 5:1). In 2 Corinthians 5:17, the apostle Paul assures Christians that "if anyone is in Christ, he is a new creation. The old has passed away; behold, the new has come."

Are you living in that newness? If not, what in your life still needs to be restored? Whatever damage has been done requires restoration through God's Word by the work of his Spirit. Let's carefully assess some areas in your life that may need restoration.

RESTORING SEXUAL PURITY

Sex was designed by God to be good. His plan for sexual intimacy was that it be enjoyed between a husband and wife exclusively. According to Genesis 2:25, we learn that "the man and his wife [Adam and Eve] were both naked and were not ashamed." They lived in openness and unhindered pleasure with no strings attached and no guilt or shame surrounding their sexual intimacy.

Sadly, their choice to sin marred their marital intimacy—including their sexual relationship. Their original sin tainted God's good gift of sex for the entire human race. Ever since the fall, our world has been ravaged by sexual sin and its consequences.

Perhaps you were sexually active outside of marriage. Maybe you have suffered sexual harassment, abuse, or assault. Adultery is also prevalent in our culture—even within the church. Pornography is easily accessible 24/7 on screens big and small. All of these things deeply impact how we view sex and sexuality. Sin—whether our own or someone else's—skews our view of God's good gift of sex.

After your abortion, you may have run to sexual partners for comfort or pleasure as I did. Using sex for selfish gain only causes more confusion about God's design for it. If you were sexually assaulted or abused, you may be terrified of ever having sex again. Sexual sin against you also distorts God's design for sex. If you have been a victim of sexual assault or sexual abuse and you are terrified of ever having sex again, I want to encourage you that God can heal even this. Not only can God renew you after the pain and trauma, but he can restore a sense of the goodness and joy of sex within marriage as he designed it to be. Several resources are listed at the end of this chapter that can help you as you seek God's healing in this area.

Think about your current view of sex. Do you have a biblical understanding and appreciation of it? Or has your abortion and the circumstances surrounding it mixed things up in your mind, causing you to disdain it? I would encourage you to seek further teaching to restore your view of sexuality according to God's Word.

God's gift of sex is sacred and is meant to be fully enjoyed within the covenant of marriage. Sexual purity is meant to be maintained in the heart of every Christian—single or married. If you are struggling to maintain sexual purity, seek the help of a Christian mentor or biblical counselor who can work with you to live in sexual purity.

RESTORATION IN MARRIAGE

Abortion can have a significantly negative impact on a marriage, even if the abortion preceded your marriage with your current spouse. In my own marriage, I was desperate to have another baby after my abortion. A fervent desire to find out if I could become pregnant again had become an idol to me. That idol wreaked havoc for the first three years of our marriage as I was fearful, demanding of my husband, and took out my fear-driven frustrations on him.

When a couple has had an abortion together, seeds of bitterness toward one another are often sown. This resentment soon sprouts like weeds in an unkempt flower bed. Bitter words and actions can choke out any attempts at constructive communication or meaningful marital intimacy. If the abortion decision was based on a dire health prognosis, the anticipation of a similar outcome in a future pregnancy can set a couple on edge. If they are dominated by this fear, they can slowly begin to distance themselves from one another.

Another inhibitor to marital intimacy is experiencing flashbacks of the procedure's physical trauma while trying to have sex with your husband. If your husband is confused as to why you are struggling to have sex, you need to ask your spouse to be patient with you. Together, you can learn how to overcome these obstacles to intimacy.

Ask a biblical counselor to help the two of you work through any hindrances. A biblical counselor can support you and your spouse in expressing Christlike love and showing patience with one another as you strive to work through any hindrances to intimacy.

PARENTING WITHOUT FEAR

As we have seen, women who have had an abortion often fear that God will punish them by permitting something bad to happen to their children in the future. If this fear is left to fester, you may struggle with either permissive or excessive parenting.

Permissive parenting rarely says no and often doesn't implement loving, yet firm discipline when necessary. This may be because you have lived under the guilt of taking the life of your preborn child. Sometimes as a form of penance, a parent will overindulge their child with an abundance of gifts or words of affirmation as a way to overcome their own guilt.

Conversely, you may be parenting excessively, what some have termed "helicopter" parenting. Are you continually hovering over your child? A parent who lives under the fear of the death or suffering of their child often implements excessive restrictions. Perhaps you rarely let your child out of your sight, or you suffer debilitating anxiety when your child isn't with you.

If either of these styles has been your approach to parenting, most likely your child will suffer mental and emotional consequences and it will hinder healthy personal and spiritual development. It is important to understand the proper balance of responsibility that parents have in caring for their children and trusting God's sovereign care over them. God is ultimately in charge of the events that take place throughout their lives (Matthew 6:25–33). He cares about you and about them; you can entrust them to him.

After examining the current state of your parenting, do you need to seek further assistance from your pastor or a biblical counselor? You can also seek the wisdom of older couples who have been parenting longer than you and appear to have a solid biblical approach to their parenting. They can be a source of parental training and encouragement to you.

As you can see, it is imperative that you have processed your past abortion experience according to the truth of God's Word and with the Holy Spirit's help and guidance. Renewing your mind with biblical truths and applying them to your life can translate to transformation in your marriage, parenting, and other relationships in need of restoration.

SHARING YOUR STORY OF CHRIST'S REDEMPTION

The goal of every Christian should be to live a fruitful life to the glory of God. If you have experienced God's healing, you should be eager to share with others God's redemptive work in you. While you do not have to tell everyone you meet, if you have experienced freedom in Christ, you will want to tell others.

Have you told your spouse or adult children about your abortion? If not, this secrecy could hinder you from sharing your testimony with someone who needs to hear that there is hope in Christ after an abortion. If you haven't already shared with your husband and children (if they are mature enough) about your previous abortion, you may shy away from telling anyone else for fear of the news getting back to your family.

You may be tempted to retreat into the shadows because of the stigma abortion carries among Christians. But once you have truly encountered the grace and mercy of Jesus Christ, your heart should be bursting to tell others about it. Two inspiring biblical accounts may embolden you to speak about your abortion as God leads you.

The Samaritan woman at the well in John 4 had a sexually sinful past and her entire village knew about it. She lived in social isolation from her community. The fact that she came to draw water from the well at noon—the hottest part of the day—indicated that she either was not allowed to draw water when the other women were there, or she did not feel comfortable being around them.

But one day, in the heat of the noonday sun, she did encounter someone at the well—Jesus. And after asking her for a drink, Christ lovingly confronted her about her past sin. He then told her that she could find "living water" in him and never thirst again. Upon hearing Jesus's good news, she shook off the shame of her past and embraced his incredible love and acceptance. No longer did she fear other people's condemnation, but the woman boldly shared her redemption story with them all (John 4:28–29). Because she chose to walk in her new identity in Christ, many others also came to faith in Jesus (John 4:39–41).

In Luke 8:26–39, we read about a demon-possessed man. Due to his mental and spiritual condition, he lived in physical isolation from his community. He was so destructive or abusive (or both) that people had tried to bind him with chains and shackles. After Jesus delivers him from the demons, he is in his right mind again. Other people could not deny the difference Jesus made in this man's life. But to him, the change in his outward appearance alone was not enough to testify to Christ's work in his life. Luke 8:39 says that he "proclaimed throughout the whole city what great things Jesus had done for him." This man wanted everyone to know about the transforming work Jesus had done on the inside!

If you have been socially or physically isolating yourself from people, especially people in the church, because of your abortion, Christ desires to transform your hiding heart. Jesus came to the earth, took on human flesh, and bore the sin of the world upon the cross. He did this so that repentant sinners could be restored to a right relationship with their Creator God.

The Old Testament often tells the history of Israel and God's restoration of his people after they commit great sins against him. On many occasions, their enemies break through their fortified walls and plunder them, and they are utterly desolated. However, God does not leave them this way.

Psalm 126 tells of Israel's response after God's restoration of their land and their possessions. This Song of Ascent can also be applied to Christians who have experienced God's spiritual restoration. It says, "When the LORD restored the fortunes of Zion, we were like those who dream. Then our mouth was filled with laughter, and our tongue with shouts of joy; then they said among the nations, 'The LORD has done great things for them.' The Lᴏʀᴅ has done great things for us; we are glad" (Psalm 126:1–3). Has God delivered you from your sin of abortion and restored you? With gladness, you too can (and should) give testimony to the great things he has done for you.

If you are not sure how to share your abortion testimony, try writing it out. Make sure to incorporate Scriptures that God used to heal your heart and renew your mind. Include how the good news of Jesus's forgiveness of your sins is central to your story.

Having your testimony in written form may make it easier to tell others about your abortion. You can either read it to them or have them read it. You could start by sharing your story with your pastor or a friend who can be trusted to listen humbly and graciously. They can encourage you and pray for you, especially if you are nervous about telling your husband or grown children.

God used James 5:16 to teach me the blessing and benefits of disclosing my sin to a trusted Christian friend or church leader. It says, "Therefore, confess your sins to one another and pray for one another, that you may be healed. The prayer of a righteous person has great power as it is working."

For me, sharing about my abortion with trusted Christian friends enabled me to grow in confidence in the freedom that I have in Christ. Each time I told someone what God had done, any residual shadows of shame over my abortion dissolved as I heard myself speak of Christ's glorious redemption. I have resolved to be obedient to share my testimony whenever God sends someone my way who needs to hear how Jesus saves sinners. Because of this, I have seen the fruit of others coming to know Christ and live in freedom from the shackles of their sin and shame.

FOR REFLECTION

1. What is holding you back from sharing with other people what Christ has done regarding your abortion?

2. If you are still uncertain about moving forward after your abortion, what next steps will you take to seek further help?

Read through these passages to reflect more on what God's Word says about living in the joy of what God has done for you. Write out one or two truths and how you will apply them to your life.

- Psalm 30:1–5, 11–12
- Colossians 3:16–17

FURTHER READING

- Linda Dillow and Lorraine Pintus, *Intimate Issues: Twenty-One Questions Christian Women Ask About Sex* (Colorado Springs, CO: Water-Brook, 2009).
- Jeff Dodge, *Gospel 101: Learning, Living, and Sharing the Gospel* (Greensboro, NC: New Growth Press, 2018).
- Martha Peace and Stuart Scott, *The Faithful Parent: A Biblical Guide to Raising a Family* (Phillipsburg, NJ: P&R Publishing, 2010).

- David Powlison, *Sexual Assault: Healing Steps for Victims* (Greensboro, NC: New Growth Press, 2010).
- David White, *God, You, & Sex: A Profound Mystery* (Greensboro, NC: New Growth Press, 2019).

KEEP MOVING FORWARD

While this book was written to help you find many answers from God's Word after your abortion, I realize that you may have more questions as you move forward. I want to point you to some additional resources as you continue on your spiritual journey. *Healing After Abortion: God's Mercy Is for You* by David Powlison (New Growth Press, 2008) is a wonderful booklet that reveals the tenderness of God and his promises to redeem your life. And I hope you will consider getting in touch with Healing Hearts Ministries International. God used their in-depth Bible study *Binding Up the Brokenhearted* to bring me incredible healing after my abortion. You can sign up to take the study with a biblical counselor who has also experienced an abortion by visiting HealingHearts.org and clicking "Get Help Now." Additionally, their Bible study *The Hem of His Garment* was written to help women who are suffering from other traumatic life experiences. If the events surrounding your abortion continue to be a difficult burden to bear, I strongly urge you to go through that study with one of their certified biblical counselors.

If you are not a Christian, but you are open to becoming one, please keep seeking to know Jesus and continue reading the Bible. God promises that those who seek him with all of their hearts will find him (Deuteronomy 4:29). I encourage you to find a Bible-teaching church that exudes both grace and truth from its leaders and its people. Seek out a mature Christian woman who is willing to walk alongside you.

And, if you have been living without much joy or purpose in your life, a relationship with Jesus is what you have been missing. Psalm 16:11 tells us, "You make known to me the path of life; in your presence there is fullness of joy; at your right hand are pleasures forevermore." Christian, these promises are for you as well.

As you have read through these chapters and have been presented with truth from God's Word, I pray that you have diligently applied it to your life. If so, along with King David, you can say, "I sought the LORD, and he answered me and delivered me from all my fears. Those who look to him are radiant, and their faces shall never be ashamed" (Psalm 34:4–5). May you continue to radiate God's love and grace to others as you tell them about the great work he has done and is doing in you.

ENDNOTES

Start Moving Forward

1. Sue Liljenberg, *Binding Up the Brokenhearted: Help for Those Suffering from Post Abortion Trauma*. Rio Rancho, NM: Healing Hearts Ministries International, 2012. https://www.healinghearts.org/get-help-now/womens-study/binding-up-the-brokenhearted/.

Chapter 6

1. *Bible Study Tools*, s.v. "Athetesis (n)," accessed October 22, 2022, https://www.biblestudytools.com/lexicons/greek/kjv/athetesis.html.

ASK THE CHRISTIAN COUNSELOR

The Ask the Christian Counselor series from New Growth Press is a series of compact books featuring biblical counseling answers to many of life's common problems. This series walks readers through their deepest and most profound questions. Each question is unpacked by an experienced counselor, who gives readers the tools to understand their struggle and to see how the gospel brings hope and healing to the problem they are facing.

Each book in the series is longer than our popular minibooks, but still short enough not to overwhelm the reader. These books can be read by individuals on their own or used within a counseling setting.

NewGrowthPress.com